Sacred Piano Preludes

Original Piano Solos for Worship Services
Volume 1

Copyright 2013

by

Kevin G. Pace

PaceMusicServices.com

Sacred Piano Preludes

Original Piano Solos for Worship Services
Volume 1

Let Thy Holy Spirit Guide	1
Were You There to Hear the Heavenly Angels Sing?	4
Mother's Day	8
Restoration Morning	11
Lord, Humbly I Come To Thee Now	16
Holy Father, I Pray	20
We'll Bow in Humble Reverence	23
Testimony	26
Sacrament	29
Come Unto Christ	32
In Reverence	36

Let Thy Holy Spirit Guide

Kevin G. Pace

Were You There To Hear the Heavenly Angels Sing?

Kevin G. Pace

Mother's Day

Kevin G. Pace

Piano

Restoration Morning

Kevin G. Pace

Lord, Humbly I Come To Thee Now

Kevin G. Pace

Holy Father, I Pray

Kevin G. Pace

We'll Bow in Humble Reverence

Kevin G. Pace

Testimony

Kevin G. Pace

29

Sacrament

Kevin G. Pace

Piano

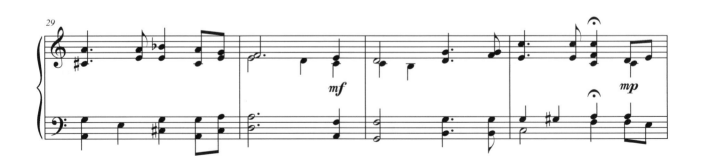

Come Unto Christ

Kevin G. Pace

In Reverence

Kevin G. Pace

Made in the USA
Columbia, SC
30 September 2023